My Long Story Short

by

John Alexander, Jr.

Table of Contents

This Inspirational Book is in Dedication to

My Father and Mother

When I was growing up, I watched my father work two jobs to support us and make sure family has everything we needed. My dad would get up every morning around 5 am to get ready for work. He worked his full time job from 7 am to 4 pm. He would come home and shower and eat dinner and leave for his part time job. Dad would work on his part time job from 6 to 11 pm.

As for my mother, a woman of support, dignity and strength in times of trouble. I use to listen to my mother sing *Amazing Grace* every morning. She would also pray and tell *God* all about it. My mother was definitely our rock, she was always there for support and guidance. Father and Mother have passed on and God has inspired me to write this book, "My Long Story Short."

The Joy of the Lord

Yes, everything the devil has stolen from me, I am taking it back. I am taking my Joy, happiness and peace, I am taking it back. *God* says in his word, this is the day I have made rejoice and be glad in it. So many times we let the devil steal our joy. Well the devil is a liar, because *God* is in control. I will not live another day in sadness or regret. I will put those days behind me, forgetting what lies behind and reaching forward to what lies ahead. I will live my days in peace and harmony. I will give all my burdens to the *Lord*. I want to live a life worthy of him. Keeping my mind on things that are pure, loving and kind. In other words, on things that are worthy to be praised.

Philippians says, "always be full of joy in the *Lord*." (Philippians 4:4 NKJV) I say again, Rejoice! Let everyone see that you are considerate in all you do. Let the *Lord* fill you with his spirit, so that others can see him shining through you. He is the only one that can give you perfect peace and joy. That is why every day and all day, I call out his name. When circumstances a rises, I turn my focus to the *Almighty*, the *Lord* of *Lord*s and King of Kings. He says in his word, if you keep your mind on me I will give you perfect peace.

So many times I have been distracted or troubled, I switch my focus to the *Lord* and all of a sudden, a chill goes down my spine, and a smile comes upon my face. Because I know *God* always has my back. It is such a joy to serve a *God* that we know is always there and upholds us with his mighty hand. He will guide us and protect us through it all. Every time I think how awesome he is I get goose bumps. Knowing and trusting *Christ* has changed my life in so many ways. I feel more at peace with myself. I wake up each morning, excited about each day, knowing that I have a *God* who loves me unconditionally. As I continue to seek him, I am more confident that whatever I face, I know everything is going to be alright. Yes, everything is going to be alright, because I am taking it all back my joy, my peace, my happiness, yes I am taking it all back and I am going to keep it. I will not let anyone steal what *God* has promised me. He says as long as I stay focused on him, these things are given. What a joy and comfort to know that these things are promised.

The Joy of the *Lord*. Let us break down the word Joy. J is for *Jesus*. O is for others. Y is for yourself. And it goes like this. If you put the will of *Jesus* first and needs of others above your own, you will find Joy. Yes, to experience this wonderful Joy, you have to have *Christ* live in you and you live in *Christ*.

When you talk about the Joy of the *Lord*, you are talking about something deep down inside. The Apostle Paul knew it best. Paul had learned the secret, he was able to experience Joy and peace in any kind of situation, whether he was surrounded by friends or isolated in a Roman prison. It is so ironic, all of us are going thru something similar with this covid-19 and the stay at home order. The Apostle Paul understood what it meant to live in *Christ* and to have *Christ* living in him. He made a simple but profound faith decision to draw his life from the *Lord* and as a result he had the calm assurance that what he possessed inside could never be stolen. Yes, the Joy of the *Lord* can never be stolen when you let *Christ* live in you and you live in *Christ*.

The Love Of Jesus Christ

First his love is everlasting and unconditional. His love is not based on a feeling. It flows from his very nature and his creation. Human love fluctuates, or fail, due to disagreements and other circumstances. There are two commandments that stand out most in the Bible. First is to love *Christ* first and the second is to love others. Let us look at these two commandments in a little more depth. If you truly love *Christ* first with all your heart, mind, soul and strength, you would want to do what pleases him. In the same way, if you really love others as you love yourself, you will be concerned for their welfare and will treat them accordingly. The book of John tells us, "For *God* so loved the world that He gave His only begotten Son, that whoever believes in Him should not perish but have everlasting life." (John 3:16 NKJV)

Further explained in the book of Romans, *God* showed his great love for us by sending *Christ* to die for us even though we were sinners without a relationship with him. (See Romans 5:6-8) He willingly took the punishment of those who tortured him, hated him, rebelled against him. He gave the most he could give for those who deserved it the least. Sacrifice, then, is the essence of *God*-ly love. This is *God* like love and not man like love.

Let us look at man-like love verses *God* like love. In man-like love, sometimes people may give their lives willingly for someone, a friend, a relative and other good people they think worthy of it. But *Christ's* love goes beyond that. *Christ* love extends to those unworthy. Remember we must trust him as our savior. In turn this makes us *God's* children. "But if Christ is in you, although the body is dead because of sin, the Spirit is life because of righteousness. If the Spirit of him who raised Jesus from the dead dwells in you, he who raised Christ Jesus from the dead will also give life to your mortal bodies through his Spirit who dwells in you." (Romans 8:10-11 ESV). We have his love and companionship forever. What an Amazing *God* we serve. *God* loves us unconditionally. Then each day as I read his word to strengthen my growth in knowing and building relationship with him, I realize the trials and tribulations I experienced. I know now it was *God's* love that brought me through it all. He never left my side and guided me through it all.

Just think of a life dedicated to *Christ*, the *almighty* and creator. A *God* that knows our every need. A *God* that we can call on anytime of the day. A *God* that looks beyond our faults and sees the good in us. A *God* that showers us with blessings each and every day. A *God* that looks from the inside out and not the outside in. A *God* that will supply all of our needs. A *God* that promises eternal life if we just trust and believe in him. A *God* that says do not worry about anything, but pray about everything. A *God* that wakes you up each morning, to see another day, so you can rejoice and be glad in it. A *God* that says if you keep your mind on me, I will give you perfect peace.

"Come to me all of you who are weary and carry heavy burdens, and I will give you rest. Take my yoke upon you, let me teach you, because I am humble and gentle and you will find rest for your souls. For my yoke fits perfectly and the burden I give you is light," (Mathew 12:28-30 NKJV).

As I continue to look back, the *Lord* kept me through the midst of my trials and tribulations. Not because I was so faithful or not because I was obedient, but because he loved me so dearly. He kept me through it all. Yes he kept me, he protected me and he brought me through the storms. Yes, the storms were raging, but *God* kept me through it all. Chills run down my spine, when I realize it did not matter who I was, what I did and what I did not do, *God* kept me through the midst of it all. This is the Love of our *Awesome God*.

Trusting In Jesus Christ

Walk by faith and not by sight, trusting *God* to open the way for you. So how do we hold on to our faith and trust *God* in times of trouble? First we have to know what faith is. "Now faith is the substance of things hoped for, the evidence of things not seen." (Hebrews 11:1 NKJV). If you really want to know what true faith is all about, let us look at the situation with Daniel. Daniel was thrown in the lion's den, because of his faithfulness to *God*. Daniel valiantly maintained his prayer times, even in the midst of persecution and punishment. He served no other idols. In all circumstances, Daniel chose to follow the commands of the *Lord*. Daniel new that *God* was bigger than his circumstances. And guess what? *God* honored Daniel's faithfulness, rescuing him from the lion's den and blessing him with great favor. Remember *God* did not promise us that we would not experience hard times, but he does say that he will accompany us every step of the way.

Let us look at Nehemiah. Nehemiah was a man of great faith and complete trust in *God*. Nehemiah had many concerns for Jerusalem. The walls had been torn down and the gates burned. But through praying for *God*'s guidance and studying *God*'s law, Nehemiah and the people of Jerusalem were able to rebuild the walls and gates of Jerusalem. Nehemiah faced many obstacles, he had many people that were opposed to rebuilding. They threatened to kill him. But Nehemiah prayed and continued to ask for guidance from the *Lord*. Every decision and every move he made, Nehemiah prayed for guidance. The *Lord* embraced Nehemiah with his favor, mercy and grace. One thing that Nehemiah did, he had all the people gather in the square, to listen to the Priest Ezra, as he read the Book of the Law of Moses, which the *Lord* had given for Israel to obey. You have to remember the joy of the *Lord* is our strength. Nehemiah new that by studying and understanding *God*'s word, this would help him and his people get through the trials and tribulations that they went through in trying to rebuild the gates and walls of Jerusalem. The teaching of *God*'s word kept Nehemiah and the people encouraged.

Let us look at a Job for a moment. Job was a man of integrity. He feared *God* and he stayed away from evil. Job was the richest man in the city. *God* had always protected him and his home and his property from harm. But Satan comes along and tries to test Job's faith and the trust that he had in *God*. Job was such an encouragement to others in times of trouble. Everyone new about Job's commitment to *God*. He was well liked in the community and as I said before he stayed away from evil. He showed kindness to all the people and most of all his family. Job loved everyone. I think Job thought that no evil could come upon him and his family. Now it was time for Job's faith to be tested. Job was about to face the biggest challenge of his life.

Before we go into what happen to Job. Let us look at what Job possessed. Job had seven sons and three daughters. He owned seven thousand sheep, three thousand camels, five hundred teams of oxen, and five hundred female donkeys and he employed many servants. Here again, *God* allowed Satan to afflict Job in order to see whether he would trust *God* in the face of affliction, or curse *God* and reject the faith. Job lost his property and possessions, his family and his health. Through two raids, Job lost most of his animals and many of his servants were killed. A fire broke out and burned all of his sheep and all the shepherds. And if that wasn't enough, a wind storm came in from the desert and hit the house on all sides. The house collapsed while the sons and daughters were feasting. They all died.

This man had accomplished so much through the first part of his life. Here was a righteous man that had integrity, and he also was obedient to *God*. Job had no idea that something like this could happen to him. Job lost hope within himself. He could not understand why all this had happened to him. To lose your family and all your possessions. Yes, he had some doubt. Even Job's friends assumed that *God* could not allow the righteous to suffer. The tragedies suffered by Job, they imagined had to be the result of some terrible sin in his life. But Job new he had not committed any sin. In his despair over his condition, and his hurt at his friend's accusations, he tried to justify himself before *God*. He could not understand *God*'s ways, so he questioned them. Job and his friends had to learn that suffering is not always the result of sin but often serves a purpose known only to *God*. "'For my thoughts are not your thoughts, Nor are your ways My ways,' says the *Lord*." (Isaiah 55:8 NKJV). We all know that *God* has a purpose for all things that we encounter in life. His ways are above our own understanding. I say this because, the *Lord* Blessed the second half of Job's life. For now he had fourteen thousand sheep, six thousand camels, one thousand team of oxen, one thousand female donkeys. *God* also gave Job seven more sons and three more daughters. Job lived to be 140 years old. He lived to see four generations of his children and grandchildren.

The Presence Of God

First *God* says, live in the light of my Presence, by fixing your eyes on me. Then you will be able to run with endurance the race that is set before you without stumbling or falling. Each day I feel his presence around me. It feels so good to know that *God* surrounds me with his blood, his love and his power. *God* says be still in the light of my Presence, while I communicate Love to you. There is no force in the universe as powerful as my love. You are constantly aware of limitations, your own and others. But there is no limit to my love; it fills all of space, time, and eternity. So being in his presence, we are surrounded by his unconditional love. Let us go a little deeper, to understand why *God's* Presence is so important. *God* says when my presence is the focal point of your conscience, all the pieces of your life falls into place. As you live in the radiance of my presence, my peace shines upon you and my presence shall go with you and I will give you rest. Awareness of my presence fills your mind with light and peace leaving no room for fear.

As I continue my journey I realize without his presence around me I am nothing. Knowing that he is with me I wake up each morning excited and refreshed knowing that I can begin another day of enjoying his presence. I can relax in knowing that he is with me throughout the day, protecting, blessing me and covering me with his blood.

The last two days with my wife at the hospital was really a test of *God*'s presence throughout the two days. From the doctors to the nurses even as far as the custodian staff, the atmosphere was radiant or should I say *God* was in this place. Everyone was so helpful in making sure my wife was comfortable throughout the ordeal. Even during the MRI in which my wife was totally against it because of being enclosed in this small tubular machine. It kind of freaked her out. Everyone was so patient and kind, it was just like putting themselves in her place. They understood what she was going through. To see a friendly smile and to see everyone being so helpful showed *God*'s presence throughout the two days. All the test came out find and my wife was released from the hospital. So when *God* is with you everything falls right into place.

One thing I realize that *God* is always in control, he will supply all of our needs. Recently I had an issue with my 1979 corvette. The windshield wipers were not working. I guess you are all wondering, where I am going with this. Well give me a minute I will tell you. Through my research I narrowed it down to the wiper relay. I installed the wiper relay, mind you when I did the installation I did it from the passenger side of the car. When I turned the wipers on nothing. So a soft voice spoke to me and said check the wiring from the driver side. When I looked from the driver side I noticed that the male plug and female plug was not connected. Connected them and the wipers began to work. So you see his presence is so important as we continue to live life. Life will throw you many curves. But the *God* we serve is bigger than anything we can imagine, and says, "I have overcome the world." (John 16:33 NKJV).

Keeping Your Eyes On Jesus

When *God* steps in miracles happen. *Jesus* tells us in the book of Revelation, "Behold, I stand at the door and knock. If anyone hears my voice and opens the door, I will come in to him and eat with him, and he with me." (Revelation 3:20 NKJV).

Yes, *God* is the way, the truth, and the life. He will always be with you in time of need. His presence is always near. You can reach out anytime and your prayers will be answered as long it is within his will. Trust him with all your mind, soul, and heart. He is there to strengthen and lead you in the right direction. Our *God* is a loving, passionate *God*, who will never forsake us. So let your troubles be his troubles, let your circumstances be his circumstances, let all your concerns be his concerns. In other words, let *God* be your life and you will walk in total peace.

Yes, keeping your eyes on *Jesus*. I realized *God* is the only certainty in this life. You can count on the one who is faithful, just, and loving. When the issue of cancer came up many years ago, the *Lord* was my rock. That was the first time in my life, that I, at that moment turn the situation over to the one who knows everything. All my life, I have tried to fix things on my own. But this one was bigger than me, I had to give this burden to the *Almighty God*. Yes, the *Lord* is my light and my salvation; whom shall I fear. I had to take refuge in the *Lord*, because He protects me. He places my feet on a solid rock and guides me through it all. Without Him, there would be no hope or security. *God* says, look at life through my eyes, do not be afraid. Stop letting life intimidate you. Stop running scared. Keep your eyes on me. Trust me! I know for a fact, perfect trust in him changes us. It does not make life all rosy, beautiful, neat , lovely, financially secure, and comfortable. But it is trust that is rooted in an abiding faith in *God*. It makes all that is real in us secure, relaxed and calm against all odds. So you see your faith is not about how strong you are; it's about how much you trust and depend on him. You don't have to be strong; you just have to be his. So *God* is the only certainty in this life. You can count on him, because he is faithful, just and loving. *Father* thank you for helping me to stay focus on you. Thank you for helping me with every struggle and calming my fears. I will trust you with all that concerns me. Amen!

God Cares For You

As I sit here in the garage, my secret place and the world has stopped because of this pandemic virus, they call covid-19. I have no fear, because I know that *God* has overcome the world. Knowing his power and goodness has given me strength to get through this pandemic virus situation. Should we fear *God* or this pandemic virus? Fearing *God* is where we need to be. His presence is protection in times of trouble. He will hide us in the midst of the storm. As I look back, *God* has brought me through so many storms in my life. This pandemic virus is no different. Faith over fear equals Grace. This is a test of faith. Believing and trusting in his word and knowing that our *God* is in control gives me perfect peace. That is why the *Lord* says pray without ceasing. Other words let prayer be consistent throughout our life. Each day we should be thanking and giving *God* all the glory, even going through times like this. If you think about it, each day is a gift from *God*. We all should rejoice and be glad in it. But instead some of us are full of hate, and no love for one another. We do not appreciate the things that *God* has given us. *God* wants us to humble ourselves and be thankful. *God*'s word is very powerful. It gives us direction and guidance for our life. Through *God*'s word, he lets us know that he is always with us through bad times and good times. With the knowledge of his word, it keeps us grounded. The word keeps us on a straight and narrow path.

Galatians talks about the fruits of the spirit, "But the fruit of the Spirit is love, joy, peace, long suffering, kindness, goodness, faithfulness, gentleness, self-control. Against such there is no law." (Galatians 5:22-23 NKJV) The "fruit" that stands out the most is long suffering. Long suffering enables us to never give up, regardless of our circumstances. *Jesus* says, here I am, I stand at the door and knock. "If anyone hears my voice and opens the door, I will come in." (Revelation 3:20 NKJV)

Yes, *God* is the way, truth and the life. He will always be with you in time of need. His presence is always near. You can reach out at any time and he will listen. Trust him with all your mind and soul and your heart. He is there to strengthen and lead you in the right direction. Our *God* is a loving and passionate *God*, who will never forsake us. So let *God* care for you. Let *God* be your life and you will walk in total peace. You see, *God* cares for you.

The Almighty

Everyday about 6 to 8 am I try to gather in my garage to meditate, read my Bible and Devotional Book. I also do a lot of praying. Some might be saying, why the garage? Well this is where my hands and *God's* hands have worked miracles in fixing my cars. From cv axles, ac compressors to restoring my 1979 corvette. I call this my prayer garage. This is my quiet place. This is one of the places where I praise *God* and give him all the glory for what he has done in my life. I bring all my cares and concerns to this place. I talk, I pray, I meditate and I glorify him in this place. Yes, all my struggles and concerns are carried to this place to be delivered to the *Almighty*. This is where I find peace, joy, before I start my day. The garage is where I get away from distractions. This is where I can get away from everyone and everything. Here is where I have that intimate time with the *Almighty*.

Yes, who do you turn to in times of trouble? The *Almighty*, the one who is perfect in all things. The one that promises never to forsake you. The one that says in Isaiah, "Fear not, for I am with you; Be not dismayed, for I am your God. I will strengthen you, Yes, I will help you,I will uphold you with My righteous right hand." (Isaiah 41-10 NKJV) You know we serve a jealous *God. God* wants us to spend time with him. I know our days can be so busy, that we look around and wonder what happen to the day. But I have found out that taking a few minutes to spend time with him is better than not spending time at all. As I spend intimate time with the *Almighty*, my life is so meaningful. In other words, each day is lived. My purpose is serving the *Almighty* and enjoying his presence. Even though I still have struggles, trials and tribulations, I have peace knowing that he is with me every step of the way.

Fourteen years ago I thought I had it going on. The *Almighty* blessed me with a the job I always dreamed about. I had a great yearly income. I was married had a beautiful home, fine cars and I thought I was living the life. But all that changed quickly. I was traveling 365 days a year, all my time was put in my career and material things. Then things started to unravel. I lost my job, my wife ended up leaving me and as it turned out I lost everything. As I look back, the *Almighty* blessed me with so much and I did not take time out of my busy schedule to spend time with him or my family. I was lost and I did not realize it. I thought I had everything that a man could have. But I was missing one thing, a relationship with the *Almighty God*. As I look back I realize that the *Almighty* has to be the number one priority in your life. Without him, there is no purpose, there is no life, because he is the way, the truth and the life. He is the beginning and the end.

Fight Doubt

Some of us live our life each and every day wondering what other people think of us. Letting our feelings controlled by what someone says about us. Or we put our stuff out there on social media, to see who will like us on Facebook or Instagram. I use to live a life based on what was said or on how someone felt about me. I took a lot of things personal, and those things that were said, made me sad. Those things that were said, made me feel inadequate and confused. Yes, my whole life was built around this world and not around *God*. I realized you do not need things of this world to make you feel good. These things will let you down and you will become frustrated and depressed.

But knowing *God* is with you is all you need to travel this journey, we call life. So many times we lose insight and our faith began to waver. We try to fix and do things on our own time, instead of having the faith and trust to turn it over to *God* and leave it there. You know throughout my life; I would try to fix things on my own. Then when I mess up and I turned to *God*. Think about how many times, we have done that. Scripture tells us to live by faith, if you want to live a joyful life. But most of the time, we let doubt creep in and steal our joy. So how do we fight doubt? First by trusting and believing in *God*. Through *God's* faithfulness and me knowing that *God* had my back, produced joy and confidence. Yes, believing but not seeing. We have to fight the doubt off and believe what we feel, even though we do not see it, it will come to fruition. But that word doubt always stays in the back of your mind. And this is part of the faith and doubt battle. I always tell this story about doubt and how Satan can interfere with what you are trying to accomplish in life. Here is that story about doubt. This young man who was having a conversation with *God*. So *God* told the young man, I want you to push on the rock. The young man proceeded to push on the rock. So Satan comes along and says, why are you pushing on that rock and the rock is not moving. The young man continued to do what *God* had instructed him to do and that was to push on the rock. So Satan comes along again and says to the young man, you are so stupid, you are pushing on the rock and the rock is not moving. So guess what, the young man gets doubt in his mind. So he goes back to *God*, and he says, *Lord* you know, I have been pushing on that rock and the rock has not moved. The *Lord* looks at the young man and says son, look at your shoulders and your arms. Look how strong they look. If you wanted the rock moved all you had to do is ask me, I would have moved the rock. So you see what happens, when you doubt and take your eyes off of *God*. You see, *God* did not want him to move the rock. *God* wanted him to build his shoulders and arms up. The *Lord* wants to give us understanding, wisdom, peace, and joy. Whereas Satan wants to confuse us, kill, and destroy. Yes, that word doubt can become a battle. But keep your eye on *God* and listen for his instructions and everything is going to be alright.

Test Of Faith

About sixteen years ago I had gone to the doctor because I was suffering with chest pains. They did some tests and told me they would have the results in a few days. Two days later, I received a call from my doctor, she stated that she needed to see me as soon as possible. From the time I received that call, I was thinking all kinds of things, but believing I was not alone in this situation. I knew *God* was not going to put no more on me than what I could bear.

The next morning, I went to her office and as I was sitting there waiting to be called, I remembered *God* saying, I am a present help in times of trouble, also in (Jeremiah 33:3 NKJV), "*God* says call to me I will answer you, and I will tell you great and mighty things, which you do not know." You know we serve an *awesome God*. He protects us and love us unconditionally. He is always by our side. He would never forsake us. All you have to do is tell *God* all about it. He will give you perfect peace, no matter what the circumstances are. So the doctor finally comes in and proceeded to tell me that they had found a mass on my liver and a mass on my kidney. Listening on I began to pray, I told *God* this was bigger than me, and I was not going to accept what the doctor was telling me. I told *God* I was going to turn this situation over to him and leave it with him. The doctor continued on to say, we have to figure out how we are going to treat this. First I was not going to accept what she was telling me, and secondly, *God* says by his stripes I am healed. In (Jeremiah 33:6 NKJV), "*God* says behold, I will bring it health and healing; I will heal them and reveal to them the abundance of peace and truth."

As the days went by I knew *God* had this. I had to believe and trust *God* on this one. I could not control what was happening. But I knew *God* was bigger than my circumstance. Knowing *God* was with me, I had no fear, that's right no fear. *God* says in (2 Timothy 1:7 NKJV), "I have not given you a spirit of fear, but of power, love, and a sound mind." Once again I go back to scripture, (Isaiah 41:10 NKJV), "don't be afraid, for I am with you. Do not be dismayed, for I am your *God*. I will strengthen you. I will help you, I will uphold you with my victorious right hand."

Few days later I was traveling to Tennessee. As I arrived at the airport, my phone began to rang. It was my doctor. As I listen, she said Mr. Alexander, I do not know what happened, we could not find anything wrong with you, in other words the mass on your liver and the mass on your kidney are no longer there. At that moment I raised both my hands and gave my *God* a big Hallelujah. So you see *God* is a healer and a comforter. What a test of faith. I did not waver I did not have a pity party. I knew *God* had my back and I knew that he would protect me through it all. I knew by studying the word and meditating on his promises, I knew *God* was in total control. He knows me and he created me in his own image. So why should I fear. We must trust and believe in him no matter what the circumstances look like. Remember whatever you are going through always let go and let *God*.

Let Go And Let God

So many times in life, you are faced with adversities. They tend to try to steal your joy. You sit and wonder, what am I going to do? Do you want to throw in the towel or just simply give up? You are crying and shaking. Then the *Holy Spirit* steps in. "This is a day the *Lord* has made; we will rejoice and be glad in it." (Psalm 118:24 NKJV). When you get in the presence of *God,* and you turn it over to him, *God* will give you peace and understanding. When you trust in him, this pleases him. But what happens, when you are faced with trials and tribulations? First of all, I have learned that our trials are not superficial or irrelevant. They are vehicles of Grace that *God* uses to bring us to spiritual growth. When problems arise, they touch the nerve areas of our security. But *God* says, he is a present help in times of trouble. In the book of Jeremiah, "Call to Me and I will answer you, and show you great and mighty things, which you do not know." (Jeremiah 33:3 NKJV) We have to remember, that in difficult times, *God* will meet all of our needs, he is always with us and loves us forever. Remember trials are fleeting, whereas our *God*s love for us is forever. So let go and let *God.*

So let's go through a scenario. Your day was ruined, you could not function, you were miserable throughout the day. You were very unhappy and displeased with yourself. You would sit down for a moment and wondered what you were going to do, tears coming down from your eyes. Second guessing yourself, trying to turn back the clock on some decision you had made. We spend time on second guessing ourselves. It seems like you going know where fast. But guess what? There is hope because *God* says in the book of Matthew, "Come to me all you who labor and heavy laden, and I will give you rest." (Matthew 11:28 NKJV) Do you know there are 7474 promises in the Bible? When you rely on the promises of *God*, you feel peace in your heart. *God* says I am *Christ* in you, the hope of Glory. So let go and let *God* fight your battles.

God wants us to let go of our problems. When your mind moves toward a problem area, you tend to focus on that situation so intensely, that you lose sight of *God*. Your mind gears up for battle, and your body becomes tense and anxious. Philippians says, "Be anxious for nothing, but in everything by prayer and supplication, with thanksgiving, let your request be known to God; and the peace of God, which surpasses all understanding, will guard your hearts and minds through Christ Jesus." (Philippians 4:6-7 NKJV) So when a situation starts to overshadow your thoughts, bring the matter to *God*. Talk with him about it and look at it in the light of his presence and let go and let *God*.

I know when I was diagnosed with cancer several years ago, I had to let go and let *God*. When I had a major career change, I had to let go and let *God*. When I was at my wits end and did not have nowhere to turn, I had to let go and let *God*. Years ago I practically lost everything, I had to let go and let *God*. I had to let *God* be my anchor. I had to lean on him. I had to open up and let him know about all my cares. I knew in order to have peace of mind I had turn it over to *God*.

Psalm reads, "But his delight *is* in the law of the Lord, And in His law he meditates day and night." (Psalm 1:2 NKJV) Yes, to be Blessed and grow in the spirit, you have to let go of all things. Especially things you have no control of, you have to let go and let *God*. Find some time to meditate on his word. This is our guide for living a peaceful and spiritual filled life. It is so important to let go of that TV for one night and get into the word. Maybe you cut off that phone or computer and spend some time studying and meditating on *God*'s word. Starting today stop worrying about how you are going to pay your bills. Get into the word and meditate and let *God* know all about it. Yes, let go and let *God*. When you are feeling tired and depressed. Remember the word says, the joy of the *Lord* is our strength. He says he will never leave us or forsake us. He says he will be with us through eternity. (Isaiah 41:10 NKJV) says, "fear not, for I am with you; be not dismayed, for I am your *God*, I will strengthen you, I will help you, I will uphold you with my righteous right hand." Yes, *God*'s word is assuring and comforting. Yes let go and let *God*.

Life Changer

Yes, *Lord*, you are a life changer. Things that I use to do, places that I use to go, people that I use to see things that I use to say. Guess what, I do not do those things anymore. Yes, you are a life changer. You changed my life. You give me love, peace and joy. You change the way I look at life. I see things more through your eyes. Yes, you changed my life, you changed me.

I woke up this morning with you on my mind, thanking you for another day. I did not have an ache or pain as I got out of my bed. As I placed my feet on the floor, I had a smile on my face, I said thank you *Lord* for letting me see another day. I know the time, I would wake up with an attitude, wondering how I was going to get through the day. Like I say *Lord*, you are a life changer. You changed all of that. I appreciate the little things in life. I realize you are the way, and without you there is no me. Yes, *Lord*, you are a life changer.

You know I use to take life for granted. Each day was built around what bar I was going to today. How much wine could I drink, or how many boneless wings could I eat. This is how I lived from day to day. But guess what *Lord*, you are a life changer. You turned my life around, and gave me a purpose for living. I had built my life around things that would not last forever. I had to renew my mind and build my life around you. *Lord* I had to build my life on your word. By the way that is my New Year's resolution, building my life on scripture and obeying it.

It is so exciting to experience the unknowns of each day. Waking up each morning, not knowing what the day might bring. Knowing that you have an anchor in *Jesus Christ*, who is always with you. Protecting, loving and providing you with all your needs. It gives you the security of knowing you are never alone. You have *Jesus Christ* as your anchor. Yes, *Jesus*, call out his name, because we know there is power in his name. Yes, *God*, you are a life changer. I would like to call it the game of life. Let us look at the game of sports. Football, Baseball, Hockey, Basketball, Golf and Bowling just to name a few. In football it might be a touchdown. In basketball, a three pointer. In baseball a home run. In hockey a goalie. In golf a birdie. In bowling, a strike. Each sport has one or several plays that would change the game.

In the game of life, we have one true source and that source is *Jesus Christ*. He is the life changer. As we journey through life, we will have many decisions to make. These decisions can change your whole life. Some decisions might be bad and some might be good. Either way they will affect you or someone else depending upon the situation. Making the right decision is critical. Sometimes you have get down on your knees and call the one that is always on call, the one that is never busy, the one that knows everything. He is *Jesus Christ*. Several years ago when I lost my job and at the same time I was going through a separation, I was at my wits, *God* stepped in and kept me through it all. *God* changed my situation to good. He is truly a life changer. When I was diagnosed with cancer many years ago, *God* also stepped in and miraculously change that situation to no cancer. Yes, the doctors went back and tested me a few weeks later and could not find any cancer. Yes, my *God* is a life changer.

I hope that whoever is reading this, remember you are never alone. The *Lord* has so many promises, that you can live your life on. Further, the book of Jeremiah states, "For I know the thoughts that I think towards you, says the *Lord,* thoughts of peace and not evil, to give you a future and a hope." (Jeremiah 29:11 NKJV) So you see he is a life changer. Fill your mind with *God*'s word so you can think his thoughts and understand his ways. Spend time with him in intimate fellowship. The more you know him, the better you can discern his voice. Draw near to him with a grateful heart, and his presence will fill you with joy and peace. No need to worry or be anxious, close your eyes and watch *God* provide. Yes, he is a life changer.

Being Whole

Being whole means being healthy in mind, body and soul. Leaving behind childish ways and embracing spiritual relational maturity. Renew your mind. Keep your mind on that which is loving, kind and worthy to be praised. "And do not be conformed to this world, but be transformed by the renewing of your mind, that you may prove what is that good and acceptable and perfect will of God." (Romans 12:2 NKJV) Stop worrying, and know that *God* is in control. Put your energy into knowing him and building a strong relationship. Enjoy this day and be thankful, do not worry about tomorrow.

Being whole. Putting your faith in the one who created you. The one who knows everything about you. The one who faithfully supplies all of your needs. The one that wakes us up each morning, giving us the opportunity to rejoice and enjoy another day. Yes, being whole, recognizing the little things, that are given to us, each and every day. Being whole is trusting *God* through this journey of life. In the book of John we find, "These things *I* have spoken to you, that in *Me* you may have peace. In the world you will have tribulation; but be of good cheer, I have overcome the world." (John 16:33 NKJV) I have to realize that this journey won't be easy. But knowing *God* has a perfect plan for me. How do I know this? Because Jeremiah says, "For I know the thoughts I think towards you, says the *Lord,* thoughts of peace and not of evil, to give you a future and a hope." (Jeremiah 29:11 NKJV) Plans to prosper you and not harm you; plans to give you hope and a future. Knowing *God* has a perfect plan for me, puts perfect peace in my heart.

Being whole, living a *God*ly life that pleases him. Being obedient, seeking and trusting in his word. I pray every day, that the *Lord* will help me to be a person of integrity. I ask him to let my words, be seasoned with grace and my actions be filled with the fruits of the spirit. I mean love, joy, peace, patience, kindness, goodness, faithfulness, gentleness and self- control. This is a very tall order, but it is all part of being whole.

Talking about being whole. My dad was a man, I really looked up to. He was so encouraging. I really loved listening and talking to him. I could confide in him about anything. He was all so positive about everything. He always told me if you could not say something good about someone, do not say nothing at all. Dad was never rattled. He never lost his temper. He was a man of a very few words. He had a calm spirit about him. Proverbs says, "He who has knowledge spares his words, and a man of understanding is of a calm spirit." (Proverbs 17:27 NKJV) In other words, whoever restrains his words, has knowledge and he who has a calm spirit is a man of understanding. Yes, this was my Dad. Dad always told me to never worry, but continue to do what is right. In other words, righteousness will carry you along way. One day as we were talking, he spoke of three things.

He said son in order to get through life successfully, he said one, treat people the way you want to be treated. Two, put your priorities in order and thirdly be a man of your word. These things that my Dad spoke to me, were things that would make me a better man, a whole man.

Yes, being whole is something that we all would want to accomplish. I realized that it is accomplish from the inside out. Digging deep down in your soul, to be the best person that you can be. Ask yourself a question, are you being whole?

Kindness

Treating people, the way you want to be treated. Yes, kindness is a fruit of the spirit. We should wear it like a necklace. I t should never leave us. It should show in our actions and in our speech. It should be part of our character. Kindness is *God*'s will for us. Kindness includes gentleness, tenderness, patience and compassion is displayed in sensitivity and helpfulness to others. Psalms reminds us, "The *Lord* is righteous in all *His* ways, Gracious in all *His* works." (Psalm 145:17 NKJV)

"Every way of a man *is* right in his own eyes, But the *Lord* weighs the hearts." (Proverbs 21:2 NKJV) Sometimes I am that man with that stubborn heart. My attitude and ways was not what *God* would call *God*ly. My whole personality was so out of character. I could not even carry on a descent conversation with anyone without having some type of confrontation at the end. As a chosen one you have to put on the armor of gentleness patience, kindness, humility, meekness, and self- control. Looking at Colossians, it states, "Let your speech always be with grace, seasoned with salt, that you may know how you ought to answer to each other." (Colossians 4:6 NKJV)

Every day as I continue my journey, I take the time to encourage someone, with an encouraging word. *God* says let your words heal and not wound. You never know what someone is going through, or what they might face in the future. Let your words be seasoned with grace. I had a young man come up to me some time ago, to tell me he had lost his wife a few weeks ago. Prior to this happening, we always talked about how great a *God* we serve. I told him about how *God* had got me through so many tough situations. We talked about the joy and peace that *God* provides. He told me that the conversations that we had about *God*, helped him get through the sudden tragedy of his wife. Yes, an encouraging word is so important, you never know how that word might impact someone's life.

This morning I sat at my kitchen table and I stare across the room at my mother's and father's photo. My mother such a beautiful lady. She died from pancreatic cancer. I remember the last time we spoke, she was in so much pain. She would always say to me, I wish *God* would just take me. And silently, I would just look at her. As I look back on that day, If I only had just taken her in my arms and assured her that everything was going to be alright. If I had showed a little more love and passion, it would have taken, her mind off of her pain and more on my loving kind word. I could not bear seeing her in so much pain. I felt sorry for myself, because I could not help her. I did not understand. All I could see was my mother suffering. But it was not about me. My mother was lying there fighting for her life. If I could have seen it through *God*'s eyes. I would have understood what my mom was going through. At that time, she needed prayer, a hug and a passionate word from her only son. The next time I saw my mom, she was lying in a casket surrounded by the color light blue. She was so beautiful, and she had a big smile on her face. My dad looked at me and said, she has been through a lot, she looks so beautiful I feel like taking her home. That moment I knew she was in a better place. My mother had a smile on her face and a look of total peace. I had not seen her look so radiant in years. I know she is truly in heaven with the *Almighty*.

The Big 70

*L*ord it is so wonderful to wake up this morning and see another beautiful day, my birthday. Yes, the big 70 is hear finally. I looked around and I began to thank you for all you have done for me. I woke up this morning with no pains in my body, I had the activity of my limbs, and I was able to speak and tell you thank you. *Lord* you have really kept me through it all. *Lord* I humble myself before you. Without you I am nothing. *Lord* as you lead me on my journey, I want it to be all about you. I want to turn my life over to you. The one who created me. The one who is the anchor of my soul. Each day as I continue to write my book, I feel you more and more in my heart. My daily walk is different. I feel at peace. Every step I take, I know you are taking it with me. Each day is a day of just thinking how good you have been to me and my family.

Yes, the big 70. The morning of my birthday, I cried because it felt so good. Physically and mentally I felt like a renewed man. I felt I had reached a milestone. I began to praise the *Lord* for allowing me to reach 70. I had to give him all the credit for sustaining me through 70 years. The day of my birthday I received so many birthday wishes. But one really stood out and it was like *God* speaking to my heart. It went something like this. Celebrating You. There is no one like you. You have gifts that only you can give the world. You have blessings others can only receive through you. The *Lord* designed every detail of who you are. You are special, you are loved, you are you and the world is blessed to have you in it. Yes, *God* was speaking to me through this person. *God* created us in his own image. There is no one like you or me. We are all special.

Reaching 70 is a very special time in my life. The *Lord* made it all possible. I never would have made it without him. The trials that I have faced and some decisions I have made have made me sad at times. But it made me understand why things happen in life. I grew up as a man, and learned to accept responsibility for my actions. It bought forth a whole different attitude and mindset. Believing in yourself and knowing that you are somebody is so important as you continue on life's journey. I had to feel good about myself and hold my head up high. Speaking and keeping my mind on things that are kind, loving and worthy. I had to learn to keep my mind on *Christ*. Let *Christ* fight my battles. One thing that really help me through this seventh year journey, I always knew that *God* was with me. I did not spend a lot of time with him, but I always knew that he was watching over me. If someone would ask me, what bought me through these 70 years, I would say recognizing his presence and believing and trusting in him.

You know I talked about the change in attitude and mindset. You know years ago I was so engulfed in what was going on in me and around me, I could not smile, I could not be happy. I had no peace within my heart. But now each day I consider it a gift. I am able to smile because of the love and joy I get from the *Lord*. As I look back on these 70 years, I cherish the memories that he has worked with me and through me those trials and tribulations in which we have gone through. For example, relationships, cancer, and almost homeless. These are some of the trials, I had to face. And my *God* prepared me and bought me through each one of them. Yes, my *God* is an *Awesome God*. Without him I could not have made it to the big 70.

Grateful.

I am so grateful to have this opportunity to settle in my secret place to have a cup of coffee and think about the *God*, who has kept me through it all. Last year I turned 70 years old. I was so elated and happy to still be here. That morning I cried, I laugh, I smiled, because I thought about those trials I had faced throughout the 70 years. Guess what, *God* was right there with me through it all. And now a year has almost passed, and I am about to turn 71.

I was thinking the other day as I prayed to the *Lord*. I was telling him how happy I was being 70. I said *Lord* I am still celebrating my seventy birthday and now my seventy first birthday is approaching. Yes 71, is another milestone, that *God* has blessed me with. I am so grateful to have the opportunity to be able to sit here and embrace the time that I have to spend with my *God*. I am so grateful for family. He has surrounded me with some great people in my life. In which I am very grateful.

My seventy first birthday is approaching and here we are, the whole world is in the middle of a pandemic crisis. Yes a pandemic crisis, covid19. So far over one hundred thousand people have lost their lives due to this pandemic. People were told to wear mask, practice social distances, and wash hands frequently. A lot of people have failed to follow protocol. And as a result, many deaths have occurred. As the pandemic continue to spike, I thank *God* every day for protecting my family. I pray every day that he will cover us with his blood and love. He has answered my prayers and I am so grateful.

Each day I meditate on his word. Trying to get to know him and to see things through his eyes. Each day is such a blessing, when you can wake up each morning to begin to spend time in his presence. Reading his word, is my security, because it gives me the opportunity to build a stronger relationship with my *Lord* and Savior *Jesus Christ*. I know without him there is no me. My soul is anchored in him and nothing else. My focus is not on this pandemic, But on the one who created me and the one knows me more than anyone could ever imagine. He has a plan for my life that goes way beyond of what is happening in the world today. He says in his word, "These things I have spoken to you, that in Me you may have peace. In the world you will have tribulation; but be of good cheer, I have overcome the world." (John 16:33 NKJV) For this I am grateful.

The World Needs Jesus

In many ways this world needs *Jesus*. First the pandemic and now a social crisis. All of this going on at the same time. A man is killed during an arrest. People are protesting around the world for change. Police brutality continues to increase throughout the world. Lives are taken every day and we think nothing of it. Now people are trying to take a stand for equal rights in this country. On top of it all this the world is dealing with a pandemic that will not go away. Yes, the world needs *Jesus*.

A few weeks ago I had a dream. A soft voice woke me up. It was bout 3 o'clock in the morning. This voice says to me you need to read Second Chronicles. I said Second Chronicles. Yes, Second Chronicles. Immediately I said to myself, I cannot forget this, I need to remember this so I can read it in the morning. Here I am wondering why The *Lord* was telling me to read Second Chronicles in the middle of the night.

The next morning, I read Second Chronicles. It talked about the Israelites and their kings following the reign of David. It also talks about how selfish leadership divides our people. If you look at what is going on with this pandemic you can see how leadership has divided the people. It has caused hundreds of thousands of deaths so far during this pandemic and we are still counting. I cannot blame it all on our leaders. I know a lot of us did not take this pandemic as serious as others. Some of us failed to follow protocol. We did not where mask or follow the guidelines on social distances. I look at two states in particular Florida and California which open back up early are now feeling the second wave of this pandemic.

So now you are wondering , why all this happening? Have we as a nation abandoned the *Lord*? One thing I do know they took prayer out of schools. Why? Because of our constitutional rights. Does that sound familiar. Constitutional rights A lot of us did not want to wear a mask, why because of constitutional rights. We are fighting for equality, why because our constitutional rights are violated. But the main thing that we need as a nation is prayer and we take it out of the schools. It seems like we have this thing we call constitutional rights twisted. My question again to you have we abandon *God*?

So many people are trying to unite throughout the country. Then there are many that are trying to divide us. Then again as I read Second Chronicles which says, "if My people, who are called by My name will humble themselves and seek my face and turn from their wicked ways. I will hear from heaven and will forgive their sin and heal their land." (2 Chronicles 7:14 NKJV)

A Blessed Man

A Blessed Man Loves *God*. He has an open heart that is not afraid, he knows how to endure sadness. He knows how to heal and forgive. He realizes that life is like taking pictures with a camera. Focus on what's important, capture the good times, develop from the negatives, and if things don't work out take another shot. One thing about a Blessed man he will never be shaken, because he is trusting the *Lord*'s plan for his life. A blessed man will be remembered forever because of his faith in *God*.

A Blessed Man knows to seek first the kingdom of *God*. He knows *God* has a plan for his life. Spend time with him and meditate on the word. Praise him and exalt him. This makes him happy. The joy of the *Lord* is my strength. Where would I be if it wasn't for my *God*.

A Blessed Man is very familiar with self-control. This is one of the fruits of the spirit. Self-control is that inner strength that is sometime hard to control. Self-control stops bad habits. It checks us. In order to have complete control, you must live and walk by the spirit.

A Blessed Man knows how to deal with brokenness. losses, disappointments, defeat, and betrayal is part of brokenness. We all experience it at some point in our lives. The soft voice would say, I am the way, the truth and the life. A Blessed Man, would live his life to glorify *God* and not a sinful seek filled for yourself life. Through brokenness, he would learn the secret of relying upon the *Almighty God.*

A Blessed Man will suit up. I guess you all wondering what is this suit up? In other words, *God* is preparing you for what is ahead. So get ready, because *God* is getting ready to open some doors. He is preparing your heart, soul and mind. You are about to be challenged and tested. You need to be ready for whatever comes your way. I know so many times, I wanted to move before *God* moves. Don't be so quick to fix things yourself. I had to discipline myself to wait on *God*. So suit up and get ready, and to be Blessed!

The Path Of Life

A person's life is not his own. No one is able to plan his own course. Life has twists and turns. Many times, we do not take the best path. The only way to follow the right path, is to follow the one who knows the way perfectly. *God* is the perfect service guide. He watches over your steps, because he desires to see your purpose full filled and his plan come to fruition. As evidence in Philippians, "Finally, brethren, whatever things *are* true, whatever things *are* noble, whatever things *are* just, whatever things *are* pure, whatever things *are* lovely, whatever things *are* of good report, if *there is* any virtue and if *there is* anything praiseworthy—meditate on these things. " (Philippians 4:8 NKJV)

We need to be consistently filled with *God*'s truth by reading, believing, meditating upon *God*'s word and applying scripture.

"In all their affliction He was afflicted,

And the Angel of His Presence saved them;

In His love and in His pity He redeemed them;

And He bore them and carried them

All the days of old." (Isaiah 63:9 NKJV)

God in First Thessalonians also tells us to "pray without ceasing," (1 Thessalonians 5:17 NKJV). If our minds are focused upon him, unholy beliefs will not be able to take root. The word is our guide book. All of us will face difficulties as we live in this imperfect world. The world sometimes can be confusing. It places us in a dark place, which entices you, but never fixing our true existence. Yet *God's* truth will bring confidence and boldness, and his spirit will direct and strengthen, enabling us to live victoriously.

Trusting in the *Lord* is the key to a good life. The *Lord* says in Proverbs:

"My son, do not forget my law,

But let your heart keep my commands;

For length of days and long life

And peace they will add to you.

Let not mercy and truth forsake you;

Bind them around your neck,

Write them on the tablet of your heart,

And so find favor and [a]high esteem

In the sight of God and man." (Proverbs 3:1-4 NKJV)

Trust in the *Lord* with all your heart; do not depend on your own understanding. Seek his will in all you do, and he will direct your paths. So you see *God* is our path. When you seek him and pray, he keeps us on a straight and narrow path. By seeking him you gain wisdom and understanding. Wisdom is a tree of life to those who embrace her. Happy are those who hold her tightly. By wisdom the *Lord* founded the earth; by understanding he established the heavens. Remember happy is the person that finds wisdom and gains understanding.

For the *Lord* grants wisdom. From his mouth comes knowledge and understanding. He grants a treasure of good sense to the *God*ly. He is their shield, protecting those who walk with integrity. He guards the path of justice and protects those who are faithful to him. Then you will understand what is right, just, and fair, and you will know how to find the right course of action every time, for wisdom will enter your heart, and knowledge will fill you with joy. Wise planning will watch over you. Understanding will keep you safe. Proverbs says, "Commit your works to the *Lord*, and your thoughts will be established." (Proverbs 16:3 NKJV) In other words, depend on God, and your plans will have success.

Finally, I would like to close with a prayer. *God* fill us with the knowledge of your will through all spiritual understanding, and let our words be seasoned with Grace. I pray this in order that we may live a life worthy of you and pleasing you in every way. Bearing fruit in every good work, growing in the knowledge of you. Being strengthened with all power according to your glorious might, so that we may have great endurance and patience. Joyfully giving thanks to you each and every day. In *Jesus* name. Amen! Amen! Amen! This is my prayer.

Final Thoughts

We all have dreams. As a young man, my dream was to travel and merchandise retail stores throughout the country. I got into retail at an early age. I first started out as a salesperson. Then I became manager of a few stores in the Richmond Virginia area. This was my journey, salesperson, store manager and merchandising manager. As store manager, in my first year, my store was most profitable store in the company. This was quite an achievement especially when you are competing against a hundred stores or more.

At the age of 55, my dream final came true. I was able to travel many states, merchandising stores. Through trust, hope and hard work, my dream became real. I would like to pause right here and say, please have a vision of what you want to be and what you want to do in life. I am a living witness. Dreams do come true.

About the Author

Old saying is you can always learn something, no matter how old you are. That is so true. In writing my first book. I wanted it to be an inspiration to who was reading it. As it turn out, it inspired me. I realized this book was actually for me also. Yes, I had to look at myself in the mirror. I was in a dark place in my life, trying to figure things out. A life built around material things, money, and status. Nothing wrong with having those things, but do not idolized or let it be the center of your life. John 8:12 says, I am the light of the world. He who follows me shall not walk in darkness, but have the light of life. At that time I was not following him, and the light was not shining on me.

Yes I was in a very dark place in my life. This book gave me the opportunity to evaluate my life. To pay attention to how I was living my life. First, I had to ask myself a question. Had I totally committed my life to Christ? No, I had not committed my life totally to Christ. The peace and joy, I needed, I could not receive from him, because my life was centered around things that were temporary. I had to understand that the peace and joy I needed did not come from the world, but only from him. I had to take self out of every situation and let God handle it. I had to seek him first in all things. Mathew 6:33 says, But seek ye first the kingdom of God, and his righteous; and all these things shall be added unto you. KJV.

Now I am in my seventies, I am finally having the peace and joy, that I have been seeking all my life. Waking up each morning excited and thankful for another day. I have this small notebook which includes scripture readings, which I have jotted down through the years. On the front, it says choose happy. Each day I choose happy. There is no substitute for happiness.

Yes in this book, I share my experiences, patience, trust, and belief. It all came from the heart. This is a heartfelt book. Now you know a little about me. Now read the book and get inspired. My Long Story Short.